INDIAN GAMES

AN HISTORICAL RESEARCH

ANDREW McFARLAND DAVIS

1st WORLD
LIBRARY
Literary Society

Indian Games

Andrew McFarland Davis

© 1st World Library – Literary Society, 2004
PO Box 2211
Fairfield, IA 52556
www.1stworldlibrary.org
First Edition

LCCN: 2004091158

Softcover ISBN: 1-59540-604-2
eBook ISBN: 1-59540-704-9

Purchase *"Indian Games"*
as a traditional bound book at:
www.1stWorldLibrary.org/purchase.asp?ISBN=1-59540-604-2

1st World Library Literary Society is a nonprofit
organization dedicated to promoting literacy by:

- Creating a free internet library accessible from any
computer worldwide.
- Hosting writing competitions and offering book
publishing scholarships.

Readers interested in supporting literacy
through sponsorship, donations or
membership please contact:
literacy@1stworldlibrary.org
Check us out at: www.1stworldlibrary.org

Indian Games

contributed by the Charles Family
in support of
1st World Library Literary Society

"There are," says Father Brebeuf in his account of what was worthy of note among the Hurons in 1636, [Footnote: Relations des Jesuites, Quebec, 1858, p. 113.] "three kinds of games particularly in vogue with this people; cross, platter, and straw. The first two are, they say, supreme for the health. Does not that excite our pity? Lo, a poor sick person, whose body is hot with fever, whose soul foresees the end of his days, and a miserable sorcerer orders for him as the only cooling remedy, a game of cross. Sometimes it is the invalid himself who may perhaps have dreamed that he will die unless the country engages in a game of cross for his health. Then, if he has ever so little credit, you will see those who can best play at cross arrayed, village against village, in a beautiful field, and to increase the excitement, they will wager with each other their beaver skins and their necklaces of porcelain beads."

"Sometimes also one of their medicine men will say that the whole country is ill and that a game of cross is needed for its cure. It is not necessary to say more. The news incontinently spreads everywhere. The chiefs in each village give orders that all the youths shall do their duty in this respect, otherwise some great calamity will overtake the country."

LACROSSE.

In 1667, Nicolas Perrot, then acting as agent of the French government, was received near Saut Sainte Marie with stately courtesy and formal ceremony by the Miamis, to whom he was deputed. A few days after his arrival, the chief of that nation gave him, as an entertainment, a game of lacrosse. [Footnote: Histoire de l'Amerique Septentrionale par M. de Bacqueville de la Potherie, Paris, 1722, Vol. II, 124, *et seq.*] "More than two thousand persons assembled in a great plain each with his cross. A wooden ball about the size of a tennis ball was tossed in the air. From that moment there was a constant movement of all these crosses which made a noise like that of arms which one hears during a battle. Half the savages tried to send the ball to the northwest the length of the field, the others wished to make it go to the southeast. The contest which lasted for a half hour was doubtful."

In 1763, an army of confederate nations, inspired by the subtle influence of Pontiac's master mind, formed the purpose of seizing the scattered forts held by the English along the northwestern frontier. On the fourth day of June of that year, the garrison at Fort Michilimackinac, unconscious of their impending fate, thoughtlessly lolled at the foot of the palisade and whiled away the day in watching the swaying fortunes of a game of ball which was being played by some

Indians in front of the stockade. Alexander Henry, who was on the spot at the time, says that the game played by these Indians was "Baggatiway, called by the Canadians *le jeu de la Crosse.*" [Footnote: Travels and Adventures in Canada, etc, by Alexander Henry, New York, 1809, p. 78, Travels through the Interior parts of North America, by Jonathan Carver, London, 1778, p. 19. The Book of the Indians, by Samuel G. Drake, Boston, 1811, Book V, Ch. III, p. 52.]

Parkman [Footnote: The Conspiracy of Pontiac, by Francis Parkman, Boston, 1870, Vol. 1, p. 339.] concludes a vivid description of the surprise and massacre of the garrison at Michilimackinac, based upon authentic facts, as follows: "Bushing and striking, tripping their adversaries, or hurling them to the ground, they pursued the animating contest amid the laughter and applause of the spectators. Suddenly, from the midst of the multitude, the ball soared into the air and, descending in a wide curve, fell near the pickets of the fort. This was no chance stroke. It was part of a preconcerted scheme to insure the surprise and destruction of the garrison. As if in pursuit of the ball, the players turned and came rushing, a maddened and tumultuous throng, towards the gate. In a moment they had reached it. The amazed English had no time to think or act. The shrill cries of the ball-players were changed to the ferocious war-whoop. The warriors snatched from the squaws the hatchets which the latter, with this design, had concealed beneath their blankets. Some of the Indians assailed the spectators without, while others rushed into the fort, and all was carnage and confusion."

Thus we see that the favorite game of ball of the North American Indians, known to-day, as it was in 1636, by the name of "lacrosse," was potent among them as a remedial exercise or superstitious rite to cure diseases and avert disaster; that it formed part of stately ceremonials which were intended to entertain and amuse distinguished guests; and that it was made use of as a stratagem of war, by means of which to lull the suspicions of the enemy and to gain access to their forts.

The descriptions of lacrosse which have been transmitted to us, would often prove unintelligible to one who had never seen the game played. The writers of the accounts which have come down to us from the early part of the seventeenth century were men whose lives were spent among the scenes which they described and they had but little time, and few opportunities for careful writing. The individual records though somewhat confused enable us easily to identify the game, and a comparison of the different accounts shows how thoroughly the main features of the game have been preserved.

Lacrosse is played to-day as follows: The number of players on the opposing sides should be equal. Regular stations are assigned in the rules for playing the game, for twelve on each side. Goals, each consisting of two upright posts or staffs, generally about six feet apart and of equal height, are planted at each end of the field. The length of the field and its bounds are determined by the character of the ground and the skill of the players. The effort of each side is to prevent the ball from passing through the goal assigned to its protection, and equally to try to drive it through the opposite goal. Under no circumstances can the ball be touched during the game, while within the bounds, by the hands of the players. Each player has a racket, the length of which, though optional, is ordinarily from four to five feet. One end of this racket or bat is curved like a shepherd's crook, and from the curved end a thong is carried across to a point on the handle about midway its length. In the space thus enclosed between the thong and the handle, which at its broadest part should not exceed a foot in width, a flat network is interposed. This forms the bat. It is with this that the player picks up and throws the ball used in the game, which should be about eight or nine inches in circumference. The ball is placed in the centre of the field by the umpire, and when the game is called, the opposing players strive to get possession of it with their rackets. The play consists in running with it and throwing it, with the design of driving it between the adversary's goal posts; and in defensive action, the purpose of which is to prevent the opponents from accomplishing similar designs on their part. As the wind or the sunlight may favor one side or the other on any field, provision is generally made for a change of goals during the match. The stations of the players and the minor rules of the game are unimportant in this connection.

The oldest attempt at a detailed description of the game is given by Nicolas Perrot who from 1662 to 1699 spent the greater part of his time as *coureur de bois*, trader, or government agent, among the Indians of the far West. It is of him that Abbe Ferland says, "Courageous man, honest writer and good observer, Perrot lived for a long time among the Indians of the West who were very much attached to him." His accounts of the manners and customs of the North American Indians have been liberally used by subsequent writers and as the part treating of games is not only very full but also covers a very early period of history, it is doubly interesting for purposes of comparison with games of a later day. He [Footnote: Memoire sur les Moeurs, Coustumes et Relligion des Sauvages de l'Amerique Septentrionale, par Nicolas Perrot, Leipzig et Paris, 1864, p. 43, *et seq.*] says, "The savages have many kinds of games in which they delight. Their natural fondness for them is so great that they will neglect food and drink, not only to join in a game but even to look at one. There is among them a certain game of cross which is very similar to our tennis. Their custom in playing it is to match tribe against tribe, and if the numbers are not equal they render them so by withdrawing some of the men from the stronger side. You see them all armed with a cross, that is to say a stick which has a large portion at the bottom, laced like a racket. The ball with which they play is of wood and of nearly the shape of a turkey's egg. The goals of the game are fixed in an open field. These goals face to the east and to the west, to the north and to the south." Then follows a somewhat confused description of the method and the rules of the contest from which we can infer that after a side had won two goals they changed sides of the field with their opponents, and that two out of three, or three out of five goals decided the game.

Reading Perrot's description in connection with that given by de la Potherie of the game played before Perrot by the Miamis, helps us to remove the confusion of the account. Abbe Ferlande [Footnote: Cours d'Histoire du Canada, par J.B. Ferland, Quebec, 1861, Vol. I, p. 134.] describes the game. He was a diligent student of all sources of authority upon these subjects and was probably familiar with the modern game. His account of the Indian game follows that of Perrot so closely as to show that it was his model. It is, however, clear and distinct in its details, free from the confusion which attends Perrot's account and might almost serve for a description of the game as played by the Indians to-day. Perrot was a frontier-man and failed when he undertook to describe anything that required careful and exact use of language. We can only interpret him intelligently by combining his descriptions with those of other writers and applying our own knowledge of the game as we see it to-day. He is, however, more intelligible when he gets on more general ground, and after having disposed of the technicalities of the game, he proceeds: "Men, women, boys and girls are received on the sides which they make up, and they wager between themselves more or less according to their means."

"These games ordinarily begin after the melting of the ice and they last even to seed time. In the afternoon one sees all the players bedecked [Transcriber's Note: Lengthy footnote (1) relocated to chapter end.] and painted. Each party has its leader who addresses them, announcing to his players the hour fixed for opening the game. The players assemble in a crowd in the middle of the field and one of the leaders of the two sides, having the ball in his hands casts it into the air. Each one then tries to throw it towards the side where he ought to send it. If it falls to the earth, the player tries to draw it to him with his cross. If it is sent outside the crowd, then the most active players, by closely pursuing it, distinguish themselves. You hear the noise which they make striking against each other and warding off blows, in their strife to send the ball in the desired direction. When one of them holds the ball between his feet, it is for him, in his unwillingness to let it go, to avoid the blows which his adversaries incessantly shower down upon his feet. Should he happen to be wounded at this juncture, he alone is responsible for it. It has happened that some have had their legs broken, others their arms and some have been killed. It is not uncommon to see among them those who are crippled for life and who could only be at such a game by an act of sheer obstinacy. When accidents of this kind happen, the unfortunate withdraws quietly from the game if he can do so. If his injury will not permit him, his relations carry him to the cabin and the game continues until it is finished as if nothing bad happened."

"When the sides are equal the players will occupy an entire afternoon without either side gaining any advantage; at other times one of the two will gain the two games that they need to win. In this game you would say to see them run that they looked like two parties who wanted to fight. This exercise contributes much to render the savages alert and prepared to avoid blows from the tomahawk of an enemy, when they find themselves in a combat. Without being told in advance that it was a game, one might truly believe that they fought in open country. Whatever accident the game may cause, they attribute it to the chance of the game and have no ill will towards each other. The suffering is for the wounded, who bear it contentedly as if nothing had happened, thus making it appear that they have a great deal of courage and are men."

"The side that wins takes whatever has been put up on the game and whatever there is of profit, and that without any dispute on the part of the others when it is a question of paying, no matter what the kind of game. Nevertheless, if some person who is not in the game, or who has not bet anything, should throw the ball to the advantage of one side or the other, one of those whom the throw would not help would attack him, demanding if this is his affair and why he has mixed himself with it. They often come to quarrel about this and if some of the chiefs did not reconcile them, there would be blood shed and perhaps some killed."

Originally, the game was open to any number of competitors. According to the Relation of 1636, "Village was pitted against village." "Tribe was matched against tribe," says Perrot. The number engaged in the game described by La Potherie [Footnote: Vol. II, p. 126.] was estimated by him at two thousand. LaHontan [Footnote: Memoires de L'Amerique Septentrionale, ou la Suite des Voyages de Mr. Le Baron de LaHontan, Amsterdam, 1705, Vol. II, p. 113.] says that "the savages commonly played it in large companies of three or four hundred at a time," while Charlevoix [Footnote: Histoire de la Nouvelle France. Journal d'un Voyage. etc, par le P. de Charlevoix, Paris, 1744, Vol. III, p. 319.] says the number of players was variable and adds "for instance if they are eighty," thus showing about the number he would expect to find in a game. When Morgan [Footnote: League of the Iroquois, by Lewis H. Morgan, Rochester, 1851, p. 294.] speaks of six or eight on a side, he must allude to a later period, probably after the game was modified by the whites who had adopted it among their amusements. [Transcriber's Note: Lengthy footnote (2) relocated to chapter end.]

Our earliest accounts of the game as played by the Indians in the south are about one hundred years later than the corresponding records in the north. Adair [Footnote: The History of the American Indians, particularly those Nations adjoining to the Mississippi, etc, by James Adam, London, 1775, p. 399.] says the gamesters are equal in number and speaks of "the crowd of players" preventing the one who "catches the ball from throwing it off with a long direction." Bossu [Footnote: Travels through that Part of North America formerly called Louisiana, by Mr. Bossu, Captain in the French Marines. Translated from the French by John Hemhold Forster, London, 1771, Vol. I, p. 304.] says, "they are forty on each side," while Bartram [Footnote: Travels through North and South Carolina, etc., by William Bartram, Philadelphia, 1701, p. 508.] says, "the inhabitants of one town play against another in consequence of a challenge." From this it would seem that among those Indians, as at the North, the number of players was governed only by the circumstances under which the game was played.

The ball, originally of wood, [Footnote: La Potherie, Vol. II, p. 126; Perrot, p. 44.] was replaced by one made of deer skin. Adair gives the following description of its manufacture: "The ball is made of a piece of scraped deerskin, moistened, and stuffed hard with deer's hair, and strongly sewed with deer's sinews." [Footnote: p. 400.]

According to Morgan the racket has undergone a similar change, from a curved wooden head to the curved stick with open network, but we have seen in the earliest description at our command, that in the days of Perrot the cross was "laced like a racket." [Footnote: League of the Iroquois. p. 298; Perrot p. 44.]

The game was played not only by the Indians of our Coast, but Powers [Footnote: Contributions to North American Ethnology, Vol. III, p. 151. Tribes of

California by Stephen Powers; The same game is described among the Meewocs in The Native Races of the Pacific States by H. H. Bancroft, Vol. I, p. 393.] found it also among the Californian Indians. He describes a game of tennis played by the Pomo Indians in Russian River Valley, of which he had heard nothing among the northern tribes. "A ball is rounded out of an oak knot as large as those used by school boys, and it is propelled by a racket which is constructed of a long slender stick, bent double and bound together, leaving a circular hoop at the extremity, across which is woven a coarse meshwork of strings. Such an implement is not strong enough for batting the ball, neither do they bat it, but simply shove or thrust it along the ground."

Paul Kane [Footnote: Wanderings of an Artist among the Indians of North America by Paul Kane, p. 190; H. H. Bancroft's Native Races, Vol. I, p. 244.] describes a game played among the Chinooks. He says "They also take great delight in a game with a ball which is played by them in the same manner as the Cree, Chippewa and Sioux Indians. Two poles are erected about a mile apart, and the company is divided into two bands armed with sticks, having a small ring or hoop at the end with which the ball is picked up and thrown to a great distance, each party striving to get the ball past their own goal. They are sometimes a hundred on a side, and their play is kept up with great noise and excitement. At this play they bet heavily as it is generally played between tribes or villages."

Domenech [Footnote: Seven Years' Residence in the Great Deserts of North America by the Abbe Em. Domenech, Vol. II, pp. 192, 193.] writing about the Indians of the interior, calls the game "cricket," and says the players were costumed as follows: "Short drawers, or rather a belt, the body being first daubed over with a layer of bright colors; from the belt (which is short enough to leave the thighs free) hangs a long tail, tied up at the extremity with long horse hair; round their necks is a necklace, to which is attached a floating mane, dyed red, as is the tail, and falling in the way of a dress fringe over the chest and shoulders. In the northwest, in the costume indispensable to the players, feathers are sometimes substituted for horse hair." He adds "that some tribes play with two sticks" and that it is played in "winter on the ice." "The ball is made of wood or brick covered with kid-skin leather, sometimes of leather curiously interwoven." School-craft describes the game as played in the winter on the ice. [Footnote: Schoolcraft's North American Indians, Vol. II, p. 78. See also Ball-play among the Dicotis, in Philander Prescott's paper, Ibid, Vol. IV, p. 64.]

It will be observed that the widest difference prevails in the estimate of the distance apart at which the goals are set. Henry, in his account of the game at Michilimackinac says "they are at a considerable distance from each other, as a mile or more." Charlevoix places the goals in a game with eighty players at "half a league apart" meaning probably half a mile. LaHontan estimates the distance between the goals at "five or six hundred paces." Adair, [Footnote: Henry, p. 78 Chulevoix Vol. III, p. 319, Kane's Wanderings, p. 189, LaHontan, Vol. II, p. 113; Adair, p. 400.] who is an intelligent writer, and who was thoroughly conversant with the habits and customs of the Cherokees, Choctaws, and Chicasaws estimates the length of the field at "five hundred yards," while Romans [Footnote: A concise Natural History of East and West Florida, by Capt Bernard Romans New

York, 1770, p. 79.] in describing the goals uses this phrase "they fix two poles across each other at about a hundred and fifty feet apart." Bossu [Footnote: Vol. I, p. 104 Similarly, Pickett (History of Alabama, Vol. I, p. 92) describes a game among the Creeks in which there was but one goal consisting of two poles erected in the centre of the field between which the ball must pass to count one. He cites "Butram," and the "Narrative of a Mission to the Creek Nation by Col. Mammus Willet," is his authorities neither of them sustains him on this point.] speaks as if in the game which he saw played there was but a single goal. He says "They agree upon a mark or aim about sixty yards off, and distinguished by two great poles, between which the ball is to pass."

The goals among the northern Indians were single posts at the ends of the field. It is among the southern Indians that we first hear of two posts being raised to form a sort of gate through or over which the bull must pass. Adair says, "they fix two bending poles into the ground, three yards apart below, but slanting a considerable way outwards." The party that happens to throw the ball "over these counts one; but if it be thrown underneath, it is cast back and played for as usual." The ball is to be thrown "through the lower part" of the two poles which are fixed across each other at about one hundred and fifty feet apart, according to Romans. In Bossu's account it is "between" the two great poles which distinguish the mark or aim, that "the ball is to pass." On the other hand, Bartram, describing what he saw in North Carolina, speaks of the ball "being hurled into the air, midway between the two high pillars which are the goals, and the party who bears off the ball to their pillar wins the game."

In some parts of the south each player had two rackets between which the ball was caught. For this purpose they were necessarily shorter than the cross of the northern Indians. Adair says, "The ball sticks are about two feet long, the lower end somewhat resembling the palm of a hand, and which are worked with deer-skin thongs. Between these they catch the ball, and throw it a great distance." [Footnote: Adair, p. 400; A Narrative of the Military Adventures of Colonel Marinus Willett, p. 109.]

That this was not universal throughout the south would appear from Bossu's account who says, "Every one has a battle-door in his hand about two feet and a half long, made very nearly in the form of ours, of walnut, or chestnut wood, and covered with roe-skins." Bartram also says that each person has "a racquet or hurl, which is an implement of a very curious construction somewhat resembling a ladle or little hoop net, with a handle near three feet in length, the hoop and handle of wood and the netting of thongs of raw-hide or tendons of an animal."

Catlin [Footnote: Letters and Notes on the Manners, Customs and Condition of the North American Indians, by George Catlin, Vol. II, p. 123 *et seq.*] saw the game played by the Choctaws, on their Western Reservation. They used two rackets. In this game the old men acted as judges.

The game was ordinarily started by tossing the ball into the air in the centre of the field. This act is represented by Perrot as having been performed by one of the leaders in the game, but it is more in accord with the spirit in which the game was played, that it should have been done by some outsider. Bossu says, "An old man stands in the middle of the place appropriated to the play, and throws up into the air a ball of roe-skins rolled about each other," while Powers [Footnote: Contributions to North American Ethnology, Vol. III, p. 151.] says that among the Californian Indians this act was performed by a squaw. The judges started the ball among the Choctaws. [Footnote: Cuthu, Vol. II, p. 12.] Notwithstanding the differences in the forms of the goals, their distance apart and the methods of play disclosed in all these descriptions, the game can only be regarded as the same. The historians who have preserved for us the accounts of the ancient southern games from which quotations have been made, are all Englishmen except Bossu, and he entered the country not by the way of Quebec but by way of New Orleans. It is not strange, therefore, that we do not find in use amongst them the name which the early French fathers and traders invariably applied to the game. The description, however, given by these writers, of the racket used in the south, corresponds so closely with the crook from which the game took the name by which it is known, that we must accept the game as a modified form of lacrosse. From Maine to Florida, from the Atlantic to the Pacific, we trace a knowledge of it. We have found it in use among the confederate nations of the north and of the south and among scattered tribes throughout the country.

In the majority of instances the natural instincts of those who participated in the strife were stimulated by local pride. The reputation of their tribe or their village rested upon the result. Ardent as the spirit of the contest must necessarily have been under such circumstances, among a people where courage and physique counted for so much, their intense passion for gambling intervened to fan into fiercer flames the spirits of the contesting players and to inspire them to more earnest efforts. Stakes, often of the utmost consequence to the players and their backers, were wagered upon the games. A reputation for courage, for skill and for endurance, was the most valuable possession of the Indian. The maintenance of this was to a certain extent involved in each game that he played. Oftentimes in addition to this, all of his own possessions and the property of his friends and neighbors in the form of skins and beads were staked upon the result of the contest. In games where so much was involved, we need not be surprised to learn from Perrot that limbs were occasionally broken and that sometimes players were even killed. In the notes to Perrot's Memoir it is stated that some anonymous annotator has written across the margin of Perrot's manuscript at this point: [Footnote: Perrot. Note 1, Ch. x. p. 187.] "False, neither arms nor legs are broken, nor are players ever killed." We scarcely need the corroboratory statements of La Potherie [Footnote: Vol. II, pp. 126-137.] that "these games are ordinarily followed by broken heads, arms and legs, and often people are killed at them;" and also of LaHontan, [Footnote: Vol. II, p. 113.] that "they tear their skins and break their legs" at them, to satisfy us that Perrot rather than his critic is to be believed. If no such statements had been made, we should infer that so violent a game, on which stakes of such vital importance were placed, could not be played by a people like the Indians, except with such results. Notwithstanding the violence of the game and the deep interest which the players and spectators took in it, the testimony of historians is uniform to the effect that accidental injuries received during its progress produced no ill will. We have seen that Perrot states that if anyone attempted to hold the ball with *his feet,* he took his chance of injury, and that those who were injured retired quietly from the field. Adair says, "It is a very unusual thing to see them act spitefully, not even in this severe and tempting exercise." Bossu bears testimony to the same effect, in the following words: "The players are never displeased; some old men, who assist at the play, become mediators, and determine that the play is only intended as a recreation, and not as an opportunity of quarrelling."

Where the game was played by appointment in response to a challenge, the men and women assembled in their best ornaments, and danced and sang during the day and night previous to that of the appointed day. The players supplicated the Great Spirit for success. Female relations chanted to him all the previous night and the men fasted from the previous night till the game was over. [Footnote: Adair, p. 401, Bossu, Vol. I, p. 306, and Willet's Narrative, p. 109.] The players wore but little in the way of covering. Romans speaks of them as being "almost naked, painted and ornamented with feathers;" and Bossu says they were "naked, painted with various colours, having a tyger tail fastened behind, and feathers on their heads and arms."

It is not astonishing that a game which called for such vigorous exorcise [Footnote: Ferdinand Vol. I, p. 134, and Major C. Swan in a Report concerning the Creeks in 1791. Schoolcraft, Vol. v, p. 277, that the Whites exceed the Indians at this game.] and which taxed the strength, agility and endurance of the players to such a degree, should be described by writers in terms which showed that they looked upon it rather in the light of a manly contest than as an amusement. Nevertheless the young people and the women often took part in it.

Perrot tells us so, and both Romans and Bossu say that after the men were through, the women usually played a game, the bets on which were generally high. Powers [Footnote: Contributions to North American Ethnology, Vol. in, p. 151.] represents the squaws among the Californian Indians as joining the game.

Dexterity in the game lay in the skilful use of the racket; in rapid running; in waylaying an adversary when he was in possession of the ball; in avoiding members of the opposing side when the player himself was running with the ball for the goal, and in adroitly passing the ball to one of the same side when surrounded by opponents. To give full scope to skill in the use of the racket, great stress was laid upon the rule that the ball was not to be touched by the hand. Perrot says, "if it falls to the earth he tries to draw it to him with his cross." Charlevoix says, "Their business is to strike the ball to the post of the adverse party without letting it fall to the ground and without touching it with the hand." Adair says, "They are not allowed to catch it with their hands."

The early writers were struck with the fact that the character of the exercise in this game was fitted to develop the young warriors for the war path, and they commented on the practice that they thus acquired in rapid running and in avoiding blows from an instrument in the hands of an adversary.

"When we review the various features of the game which its chroniclers have thought worthy of record, we can but conclude that it was rather a contest of grave importance to the players than a mere pastime, nor can we fail to accept the concurrent testimony as to the widespread territory in which it was domesticated, as additional evidence of the extent of the intercourse which prevailed among the native tribes of this country."

[Relocated Footnote (1): I translate *apiffez*, "bedecked," assuming from the context that the author meant to write "*attifez*." We have, elsewhere, accounts which show that ballplayers, even though compelled to play with scant clothing, still covered themselves with their ornaments. J. M. Stanley in his Portraits of North American Indians, Smithsonian Miscellaneous Collections, Washington, 1862, Vol. II, p. 13, says that the "Creek" ball-players first appear on the ground in costume. "During the play they divest themselves of all their ornaments which are usually displayed on these occasions for the purpose of betting on the result of the play."]

[Relocated Footnote (2): The game is also mentioned in An Account of the Remarkable Occurrences in the Life and Travels of Col. James Smith during his Captivity with the Indians in the years 1755-1759. Cincinnati, 1870, p. 78. It is described by Col. William L. Stone in his Life of Brant, Albany, 1865, Vol. II, p. 448. In one game of which he speaks, the ball was started by a young and beautiful squaw who was elaborately dressed for the occasion. Notwithstanding the extent and value of Col. Stone's contributions to the literature on the subject of the North American Indians, he makes the erroneous statement that "The Six Nations had adopted from the Whites the popular game of ball or cricket" See p. 445, same volume, *cf.* The Memoir upon the late War in North America, 1755-1760, by M. Pouchot, translated and edited by Franklin B. Hough, Vol. II, p. 195. A game of ball is also described in Historical Collections of Georgia, by the

Rev. George White, 3d edition, New York, 1835, p. 670, which took place in Walker County, Georgia, between Chatooga and Chicamauga. The ball was thrown up at the centre. The bats were described as curiously carved spoons. If the ball touched the ground the play stopped and it was thrown up again. Rev. J. Owen Dorsey in a paper entitled "Omaha Sociology," printed in the Third Annual Report of the Bureau of Ethnology, etc, 1881-1882, Washington, 1884 p. 230, p. 336, describes the game amongst the Omahas.]

PLATTER OR DICE.

The second in the list of games given by Father Brebeuf is that which he calls "platter." Writers who describe the habits of the Indians at the north have much to say concerning this game. According to Lescarbot, Jacques Cartier saw it played, and recorded his observations. [Footnote: Histoire de la Nouvelle France par Marc Lescarbot, Nouvelle Edition, Paris 1856, Vol. III, p. 734.]

Sagard Theodat [Footnote: Histoire du Canada, etc., par Gabriel Sagard Theodat; Nouvelle Edition, Paris, 1856, Vol. I, pp. 243-244.] devotes considerable space to it. Both Father Brebeuf, in his Relation in 1636, and Father Lalemant, in his Relation in 1639, give long accounts of the game, the causes for its being played, the excesses in gambling to which it leads, and the methods which prevail in its practice. In Perrot's [Footnote: p. 50.] work there is a good description of the game, although not so full as his account of lacrosse, from which we have already quoted. La Potherie and LaHontan barely mention it. Latitau [Footnote: Mours des Sauvages Ameriquains, erc, par le P. Latitau, Paris, 1724, Vol. II, p. 339.] in his searching analysis of the manuscripts deposited at Quebec, while seeking for traces of his theory that a resemblance existed between the habits of the Indians and those of the ancient dwellers in eastern Europe, found an unusual quantity of material bearing on this particular topic, which he has reproduced in his book. Charlevoix [Footnote: Vol. III, pp. 260-1.], in a letter dated June 8, 1721, says, "As I was returning through a quarter of the Huron village, I perceived a number of these Indians, who seemed much heated at play. I approached them and found that the game they were playing at was what they called the game of platter. This is the game to which the Indians are addicted above all others. They sometimes lose their rest and in some degree their very senses at it. They stake all they are worth, and several of them have been known to continue at it till they have stript themselves stark naked and lost all their movables in their cabin. Some have been known to stake their liberty for a certain time. This circumstance proves beyond all doubt how passionately fond they are of it, there being no people in the world more jealous of their liberty than our Indians."

In the description which Charlevoix then gives, he is relied partly upon personal observations and also to some extent, upon accounts which were at that time in manuscript in Quebec mid which were easily accessible to him. He was himself an intelligent observer and a cultivated man. His history and his letters, although not free from the looseness of expression which pervades contemporaneous accounts show on the whole the discipline of an educated mind. We learn from him and from the authorities heretofore enumerated that two players only from each side could participate in this game at any given time during its progress. The necessary implements were a bowl and a number of dice fashioned somewhat like apricot seeds, and colored differently upon the upper and lower sides. Generally, one side was white and the other black. The number of these dice was generally six. There was no fixed rule as to the materials of which they were made; sometimes they were of bone; sometimes the stones of fruits were used. The important point was that the centre of gravity of each die should be so placed, that when it was thrown into the air, or when the bowl in which it was placed, was violently twirled, there would be an even chance as to which of its two sides the die would settle upon when it lodged; and in the game as it was played in early times that the whole number of dice used should be uniform in the coloring of the sides, each die having the different sides of different colors. The dice were placed in the bowl which was generally of wood, between the two players who were to cast them in behalf of their respective sides. These casters or throwers were selected by each side and the prevailing motives in their choice were generally based upon some superstitious belief in their luck. Perhaps this one had dreamed that he would win. Perhaps that one was believed to possess some magic power, or some secret ointment which when applied to the dice would cause them to turn up favorably for his side. [Footnote: Relations des Jesuites, Relation en l'Annue, 1636, p. 113.] The spectators were generally arranged in seats along the sides of the cabin [Footnote: Ibid, Relation en l'Annue, 1639, p. 95.], placed in tiers so that each person could have a view of the players. They were in more senses than one deeply interested in the game. When the cast was to be made the player would strike the bowl upon the ground so as to make the dice jump into the air [Footnote: Sigud Theodat Vol. 1, p. 213.] and would then twirl the bowl rapidly around. During this process and until it stopped its revolutions and the dice finally settled, the players addressed the dice and beat themselves on their breasts. [Footnote: Shea's Hennepin, p. 300.] The spectators during the same period filled the air with shouts and invoked aid from their own protecting powers, while in the same breath they poured forth imprecations on those of their adversaries. The number of points affected the length of the game and as entirely optional. If six dice were used and all came up of the same color, the throw counted five. [Footnote: Among the Delawares it required eight counts of five to win. History of the Mission of the United Brethren among the Indians etc. G H Loskiel. Translated by I Latrobe, Part I, Ch. VIII, p. 106.] If five of them were of the same color it counted one. Any lower number failed to count. If the caster was unsuccessful he gave place to another, but so long as he continued to win his side would retain him in that position. [Footnote: Charlevoix Vol. III, p. 264.] The game was often ushered in with singing. Like lacrosse it was prescribed as a remedy for sickness or in consequence of dreams, and the sufferer in whose behalf the game was played was borne to the cabin in which it was to take place. Preliminary fasting and continence were observed, and every effort made that superstition could suggest to discover who would be the lucky thrower and who could aid the caster by his presence at the contest. Old men, unable to walk thither, were brought up on the shoulders of the young men that their presence might be propitious to the chances of the game. [Footnote: Ibid p. 202.] The excitement which attended one of these games of chance was intense, especially when the game reached a critical point and some particular throw was likely to terminate it. Charlevoix says the games often lasted for five or six days [Footnote: Loskiel (p. 106) saw a game between two Iroquois towns which lasted eight days. Sacrifices for luck were offered by the sides each night.] and oftentimes the spectators concerned in the game, "are in such an agitation as to be transported out of themselves to such a degree that they quarrel and fight, which never happens to the Hurons, except on these occasions or when they are drunk."

Perhaps rum was responsible also for these quarrels; for in the early accounts we are told that losses were philosophically accepted. Father Biebeuf tells of a party who had lost their leggings at one of these games and who returned to their village in three feet of snow as cheerful in appearance as if they had won. There seems to have been no limit to which they would not go in their stakes while under the excitement of the game. Clothing, wife, family and sometimes the personal liberty of the player himself rested in the hazard of the die. [Footnote: Cheulevoix Vol. III, p. 261. Le Grand Voyage du Pays Des Hurons, pan Gabriel Sigud Theodat Puis 1632, Nouvelle Edition, Paris, 1835, p. 85, Relations de Jesuites, Relation de la Nouvelle France en l'Annee 1639, pp. 95-96, Lafitau, Vol. II, p. 341.]

The women often played the game by themselves, though apparently with less formality than characterized the great matches. The latter frequently assumed the same local characteristics that we have seen in the game of lacrosse, and we hear of village being pitted against village as a frequent feature of the game. [Footnote: Penot p. 43, Histoire du Canada par F. X. Garneau, Vol. I, p. 115.]

Morgan [Footnote: League of the Iroquois, p. 602.] describes a game played by the Iroquois with buttons or dice made of elk-horn, rounded and polished and blackened on one side. The players spread a blanket on the ground; and the dice were tossed with the hand in the air and permitted to fall on the blanket. The counts were determined as in the game of platter by the color of the sides of the dice which were exposed when they settled. The number of the dice was eight.

In Perrot's [Footnote: Periot, p. 50.] description of the game of platter he, alludes to a game, played with eight dice, on a blanket in precisely this way, but he adds that it was practised by women and girls. La Potherie [Footnote: La Potherie, Vol. III, p. 23.] says that the women sometimes play at platter, but ordinarily they cast the fruit stones with the hand as one throws dice.

Under the name of "hubbub" this game has also been described by observers among the Abenakis. Ogilby [Footnote: America, being an Accurate Description of the New World, etc. Collected and Translated by John Ogilby. London, 1670, Book II, Ch. II, p. 155.] says: "Hubbub is five small Bones in a small Tray; the Bones be like a Die, but something flatter, black on the one side and white on the other, which they place on the Ground, against which violently thumping the Platter, the Bones mount, changing Colour with the windy whisking of their Hands to and fro; which action in that sport they much use, smiting themselves on the Breasts and Thighs, crying out Hub Hub Hub; they may be heard playing at this game a quarter of a mile off. The Bones being all black or white make a double Game; if three of one colour, and two of another, then they afford but a single game; four of a colour and one differing is nothing. So long as the Man wins he keeps the Tray, but if he lose the next Man takes it."

There is but little said about this game in the south by writers. It evidently had no such hold there as among the Hurons and the tribes along the Lakes. Lawson

[Footnote: History of North Carolina by John Lawson, London, 1718, p. 176.] saw it played in North Carolina with persimmon stones as dice. While this fixes the fact that the game had a home among the southern Indians, the way in which it has been slighted by the majority of writers who treat of that section shows that it was not a favorite game there.

To what shall we ascribe this? Its hold upon the northern Indians shows that it was peculiarly adapted to the temperament of the natives, and we should naturally expect to find it as much in use among the tribes of the south as with those of the north. An explanation for this may possibly be found in the difference of the climate. The game was especially adapted for the winter, and while its practice was evidently not exclusively confined to that season, it is possible that its greater hold upon the affections of the Indians of the north arose from their being obliged to resort to in-door amusements during the protracted winters in that region. From this necessity the southern Indians being in a measure exempt, they continued their out-door games as usual and never became so thoroughly infatuated with this game.

Informal contests were often held between players, in which the use of the bowl or platter was dispensed with. The dice were held in the hand and then tossed in the air. They were allowed to fall upon some prepared surface, generally a deerskin spread for the purpose. The same rules as to the color of the surfaces of the dice when they settled in their places governed the count. This form of the game is sometimes described as a separate game. Boucher [Footnote: True and Genuine Description of New France, etc, by Pierre Boucher, Paris, 1644 Translated under title "Canada to

Andrew McFarland Davis

the Seventeenth Century," Montreal, 1883, p. 57.] calls it *Paquessen*. [Footnote: Played by women and girls. Sagard Theodat, Histoire du Canada, Vol. I, p. 244.] The women of Oregon played it with marked beaver teeth. [Footnote: Contributions to North American Ethnology, Vol. I, p. 206, George Gibbs; H. H. Bancroft's Native Races, Vol. I, p. 244, The Northwest Coast by James G. Swan, p. 158.] Among the Twanas it was played with beaver or muskrat teeth. [Footnote: Bulletin U S Geological Survey, Vol. III, No. 1, April 5, 1877. Rev. M. Eels.] Powers [Footnote: Contributions to North American Ethnology, Vol. III, p. 332.] says that among the Nishmams, a tribe living on - the slopes of the Sierra Nevada between the Yuba and Cosumnes rivers, a game of dice is played by men or women, two, three or four together. The dice, four in number, consist of two acorns split lengthwise into halves, with the outsides scraped and painted red or black. They are shaken in the hand and thrown into a wide flat basket, woven in ornamental patterns. One paint and three whites, or *vice versa*, score nothing; two of each score one; four alike score four. The thrower keeps on throwing until he makes a blank throw, when another takes the dice. When all the players have stood their turn, the one who has scored the most takes the stakes."

The women of the Yokuts, [Footnote: Contributions to North American Ethnology, Vol. III, p. 377.] a Californian tribe which lived in the San Joaquin valley near Tulare Lake, had a similar game. Each die was half a large acorn or walnut shell filled with pitch and powdered charcoal and inlaid with bits of bright colored abaloni shell. Four squaws played and a fifth kept tally with fifteen sticks. There were eight dice and they scooped them up with their hands and dashed them into the basket, counting one when two or five flat surfaces turned up.

Schoolcraft [Footnote: Schoolcraft's Indian Tribes, Vol. II, pp. 71, 72.] says "one of the principal amusements of a sedentary character is that of various games, success in which depends on luck in numbers. These games, to which both the prairie and forest tribes are addicted, assume the fascination and intensity of gambling; and the most valued articles are often staked upon the luck of a throw. For this purpose the prairie tribes commonly use the stones of the wild plum or some analogous fruit, upon which various devices indicating their arithmetical value are burned in, or engraved and colored, so as at a glance to reveal the character of the pieces." Among the Dacota tribes this is known by a term which is translated the "game of plum stones." He gives illustrations of the devices on five sets of stones, numbering eight each. "To play this game a little orifice is made in the ground and a skin put in it; often it is also played on a robe." [Footnote: Domenech. Vol. II, p. 191, First Annual Report of Bureau of Ethnology. Smithsonian, 1881, p. 195.] The women and the young men play this game. The bowl is lifted with one hand and rudely pushed down to its place. The plum stones fly over several times. The stake is first put up by all who wish to play. A dozen can play at once if desirable.

Schoolcraft [Footnote: Vol. n, p. 72.] describes still another form of, the game which he found among the Chippewas, in which thirteen pieces or dice were used. Nine of them were of bone and were fashioned in figures typifying fish, serpents, etc. One side of each was painted red and had dots burned in with a hot iron. The brass pieces were circular having one side convex and the other concave. The convex side was bright, the concave dark or dull. The red pieces were the winning pieces and each had an arithmetical value. Any number of players might play. A wooden bowl, curiously carved and ornamented, was used. This form of the game may have been modified by contact with the whites. It seems to be the most complex [Footnote: See also a simpler form of the game described by Philander Prescott among the Dacotas - Schoolcraft, Vol. IV, p. 64. The tendency of the modern Indians to elaborate the game may be traced in the description of "Plumstone shooting" given in "Omaha Sociology" by Rev. J. Owen Dorsey. Third Annual Report of the Bureau of Ethnology to the Secretary of the Smithsonian Institution. Washington, 1884, p. 335.] form in which the game appears. The fact still remains however, that in some form or other we find the game in use across the entire breadth of the continent. [Footnote: Col. James Smith describes the game among the Wyandots. An Account of the Remarkable Occurrences in the Life and Travels of Col. James Smith, during his Captivity with the Indians in the Years 1755-1759. Cincinnati, 1870, p. 46. Tanner also describes it. He calls it *Beg-ga sah* or dice. Tanner's Narrative, New York, 1830, p. 114.]

STRAW OR INDIAN CARDS.

The third game mentioned by Father Brebeuf was that which was called straw. We have seen that the first of these games called for strength, agility and endurance. It was as free from elements of chance as any human contest can be. The victory belonged to the side which counted amongst its numbers those players who were the fleetest runners, the most skilful throwers and the most adroit dodgers. The second was purely a game of chance. If honestly played no other element entered into its composition. The third which we are now about to consider was much more complicated in its rules than either of the others. It closely resembled in some respects several of our modern gambling games. The French found it very difficult to comprehend and hence the accounts of it which they have given are often confused and perplexing. Boucher [Footnote: p. 57.] says, "Our French people have not yet been able to learn to play it well; it is full of spirit and these straws are to the Indians what cards are to us." Lafitau [Footnote: Vol. II, p. 351.] after quoting from Boucher says, "Baron de LaHontan also made out of it a game purely of the mind and of calculation, in which he who best knows how to add and subtract, to multiply and divide with these straws will surely win. To do this, use and practice are necessary, for these savages are nothing less than good calculators."

"Sieur Perrot, who was a celebrated traveller, and that European whom the savages of New France have most honored, left a description of this game in his manuscript Memorial. I would gladly have inserted it here but it is so obscure that it is nearly unintelligible." Charlevoix admits that he could understand nothing of the game, except as played by two persons in its simplest form and adds that he was told that "there was as much of art as of chance in the game and that the Indians are great cheats at it." [Footnote: Charlevoix, Vol. III, p. 319, Father Tailban who edited Perrot says he has not been any more successful than his predecessors and the game of straws remains to him an unsolved enigma. Perrot, Notes to Ch. X, p. 188.] Where Lafitau and Charlevoix, aided by opportunities to investigate the game itself, have failed, it would seem to be useless for us to attempt. Perrot has indeed succeeded in making his account hopelessly involved. There is however much information to be derived from it and the obscure points are after all unimportant unless one should actually wish to reproduce the game in practice. In that event there are many points connected with the counts which would prove troublesome.

To play the game, a number of straws or reeds uniform in size and of equal length were required. They were generally from six to ten inches long. The number used in the game was arbitrary. Lawson puts it at fifty-one. Charlevoix at two hundred and one. The only essential points were that the numbers should be odd and that there should be enough of them so that when the pile was divided into two parts, a glance would not reveal which of the two divisions contained the odd number of straws. In its simplest form, the game consisted, in separating the heap of straws into two parts, one of which each player took, and he whose pile contained the odd number of straws was the winner. Before the division was made the straws were subjected to a manipulation, somewhat after the manner of shuffling cards. They were then placed upon the deer-skin or upon whatever other article was selected as a surface on which to play. The player who was to make the division into two heaps, with many contortions of the body and throwing about of the arms, and with constant utterances to propitiate his good luck, would make a division of the straws with a pointed bone or some similar instrument, himself taking one of the divisions while his adversary took the other. They would then rapidly separate the straws into parcels numbering ten each and determine from the fractional remainders, who had the odd number. The speed with which this process of counting was carried on was always a source of wonder to the lookers-on, and the fact that the counting was done by tens is almost invariably mentioned. Between two people betting simply on the odd number no further rules were necessary. To determine which had the heap containing the odd number, there was no need to foot up the total number of tens. It was to be settled by what was left over after the last pile of complete tens was set aside. The number itself might be either one, three, five, seven or nine. In the more complicated form of the game, this led to giving different values to these numbers, the nine being always supreme and the one on which the highest bets were wagered. It was generally understood that the holder of this number swept the board taking all bets on other numbers as well as those on the nine. It was easy to bet beads against beads and skins against skins, in a simple game of odd or even, but when the element of different values for different combinations was introduced, some medium of exchange was needed to relieve the complications. Stones of fruit were employed just as chips or counters are used in modern gambling games, and a regular bank was practically instituted. Each player took a certain number of these counters, as the equivalent of the value of the merchandise which he proposed to hazard on the game, whether it was a gun, a blanket, or some other article. Here we have all the machinery of a regular gambling game at cards, but the resemblance does not stop here. The players put up their bets precisely as they now do in a game of faro, selecting their favorite number and fixing the amount, measured in the standard of the game, which they wished to hazard. "By the side of the straws which are on the ground are found the (*grains*) counters," says Perrot, "which the players have bet on the game." In another place, the method of indicating the bets is stated as follows: "he (meaning apparently the one who has bet) is also obliged to make two other heaps. In one he will place five, in the other seven straws, with as many (*grains*) counters as he pleases." These phrases may fairly be interpreted to mean that a record of the bets, somewhat of the same style as that kept with counters upon a faro table, was constantly before the players. Complicated rules determined when the players won or lost; when the bets were to be doubled and when they were to abide the chance of another count. The loser at the game, even after all that he had with him was gone, was sometimes permitted to continue the game on his promise to pay. If ill luck still pursued him the winner could refuse him credit and decline to play for stakes that he could not see.

The game often lasted for several days, one after another of the sides relieving his comrades at the play until one of the two sides had lost everything, it being, says Perrot, [Footnote: p. 19.] "a maxim of the savages not to quit play until one side or the other had lost everything." Those who had bet at the game had the right to substitute any person whom they pleased to play for them. "Should any dispute arise on this point," says Perrot, "between the winners and the losers, the disputants backed by their respective sides would probably come to blows, blood would be shed and the whole thing would be very difficult to settle." Cheating often took place at this game. Its exposure was considered praiseworthy and its practice denounced. If doubts were expressed as to the accuracy of a count, the matter was peacefully adjusted by a re-count by two of the spectators.

"This game of straw," says Perrot, from whose account we have made the foregoing digest, "is ordinarily held in the cabins of the chiefs, which are large, and are, so to speak, the Academy of the Savages." He concludes his account with the statement that the women never play it. [Footnote: See also Shea's Hennepin, p. 300.] The authority on this game whom Ogilby quotes slides over the difficulties of the description with the statement that "many other whimsies be in this game which would be too long to commit to paper." Abbe Ferland [Footnote: Vol. I, p. 134.] epitomizes the results of his investigation of this game as follows: "Memory, calculation and quickness of eyesight were necessary for success."

Like the game of dice or platter it was essentially a house game, and like platter it is rarely mentioned by writers who describe the habits of Indians in the south. Lawson describes it, but in slightly modified form, as follows: "Indian Cards. Their chiefest game is a sort of Arithmetick, which is managed by a parcel of small split reeds, the thickness of a small Bent; these are made very nicely, so that they part, and are tractable in their hands. They are fifty-one in number, their length about seven inches; when they play, they throw part of them to their antagonist; the art is, to discover, upon sight, how many you have, and what you throw to him that plays with you. Some are so expert at their numbers, that they will tell ten times together, what they throw out of their hands. Although the whole play is carried on with the quickest motion it is possible to use, yet some are so expert at this Game, as to win great Indian Estates by this Play. A good set of these reeds, fit to play withal are valued and sold for a dressed doe-skin."

A. W. Chase [Footnote: Overland Monthly, Vol. II, p. 433. Dorsey found a survival of the game in use among the Omahas. He called it "stick counting." Third Annual Report, Bureau of Ethnology, p. 338.] speaks of "native games of cards among the Coquelles and Makneatanas, the pasteboards being bundles of sticks." He furnishes no description of the games, but uses the same phrase which was applied by Lawson in North Carolina and by Boucher in Canada.

Frank H. Cushing [Footnote: The Century, Vol. XXVI, p. 38. My Adventures in Zuni.] speaks of a game of "Cane-cards" among the Zuni which he says "would grace the most civilized society with a refined source of amusement." He was not able fully to comprehend it.

In the list of games, there is none of which we have any detailed account, which compares with straws as played by the northern tribes, in elaborateness of construction. The unfortunate confusion which prevails throughout Perrot's description of the method of counting, and the way in which the point was shirked by all other writers on the subject, prevents any attempt at analysis. So far as we can see, the rules were arbitrary and not based upon any calculations of the laws of chance. If some other detailed account of the game should be discovered it would be interesting to follow up this question and ascertain how far the different combinations which affected the counts were based upon a theory of probabilities and how far they were arbitrary.

It will of course be noticed that the game described by Lawson was relieved from much of this complication. The dexterity required to make a throw of such a nature that the player could tell exactly the number of reeds with which he had parted, was of course remarkable and naturally called forth expressions of surprise. But there were apparently no other combinations resting upon the throw than the simple guess at the number thrown. Travellers in California have described the game in still simpler form in which we see hints of the more complex game. Here the "sticks" were thrown in the air and an immediate guess was made whether the number thrown was odd or even. An umpire kept the account with other sticks and on this count the bets were adjusted. [Footnote: Kotzebue, A Voyage of Discovery, etc. London, 1821, Vol. I, p. 282 and Vol. III, p. 44. note. W. H. Emory, U S. and Mexican Boundary Survey, Vol. I, p. 111, says: "The Yumas played a game with sticks like jackstraws." Stanley, Smithsonian Miscellaneous Collections. Vol. II, p. 55, gives among his "Portraits of North American Indians," a picture of a game which he describes as "played exclusively by women. They hold in their hands twelve sticks about six inches in length which they drop upon a rock. The sticks that fall across each other are counted for game."]

Wherever we find it and whatever the form in use, whether simple or complicated, like games of lacrosse and platter the occasion of its play was but an excuse for indulgence in the inveterate spirit of gambling which everywhere prevailed.

CHUNKEE OR HOOP AND POLE.

Among the Indians at the south, observers noted and described a game of great antiquity, of which we have no record during historical times among those of the north, unless we should classify the game of javelin described by Morgan [Footnote: League of the Iroquois, p. 300.] as a modified form of the same game. The general name by which this game was known was chunkee. When Iberville arrived at the mouth of the Mississippi he despatched a party to explore the river. The officer who kept the "Journal de la fregate, le Marin" was one of that party and he recorded the fact that the Bayagoulas and Mougoulachas passed the greater part of their time in playing in this place with great sticks which they throw after a little stone, which is nearly round and like a bullet. [Footnote: Maigry, Deconvertes, etc., Vol. 4, p. 261.] Father Gravier descended the river in 1700 and at the village of Houmas he saw a "fine level square where from morning to night there are young men who exercise themselves in running after a flat stone which they throw in the air from one end of the square to the other, and which they try to have fall on two cylinders that they roll where they think the stone will fall." [Footnote: Shea's Early Voyages. Albany, 1861, p. 143.] Adair gives the following description of the same game: "The warriors have another favorite game, called *'chungke'*, which, with propriety of language may be called 'Running hard labour.' They have near their state house [Footnote: Consult E G Squire - Aboriginal Monuments of N.Y. Smithsonian Contributions to Knowledge, Vol. II, pp. 1356 and note p. 136.] a square piece of ground well cleaned, and fine sand is carefully strewed over it, when requisite, to promote a swifter motion to what they throw along the surface. Only one or two on a side play at this ancient game. They have a stone about two fingers broad at the edge and two spans round; each party has a pole of about eight feet long, smooth, and tapering at each end, the points flat. They set off abreast of each other at six yards from the end of the playground; then one of them hurls the stone on its edge, in as direct a line as he can, a considerable distance toward the middle of the other end of the square. When they have run a few yards, each darts his pole anointed with bears' oil, with a proper force, as near as he can guess in proportion to the motion of the stone, that the end may lie close to the stone. When this is the case, the person counts two of the game, and, in proportion to the nearness of the poles to the mark, one is counted, unless by measuring, both are found to be at an equal distance from the stone. In this manner, the players will keep running most part of the day, at half speed, under the violent heat of the sun, staking their silver ornaments, their nose-, finger-and ear-rings; their breast-, arm-and wrist-plates, and even all their wearing apparel, except that which barely covers their middle. All the American Indians are much addicted to this game, which to us appears to be a task of stupid drudgery; it seems, however, to be of early origin, when their forefathers used diversions as simple as their manners. The hurling stones they use at present were from time immemorial rubbed smooth on the rocks and with prodigious labor; and they are kept with the strictest religious care, from one generation to another, and are exempted from being buried with the dead. They belong to the town where they are used, and are carefully preserved." [Footnote: See also Historical Collection, Louisiana and Florida. B. F. French (Vol. II.), second series, p. 74, New York, 1875.]

Lieut. Timberlake [Footnote: Memoirs of Lieut. Henry Timberlake, etc., London, 1765, p. 77.] describes the game as he saw it played among the Cherokees where it was known by the name of "Netteeawaw." "Each player has a pole about ten feet long, with several marks or divisions. One of them bowls a round stone with one flat side, and the other convex, on which the players all dart their poles after it, and the nearest counts according to the vicinity of the bowl to the marks on his pole."

Romans saw it among the Choctaws. He says, "The manner of playing the game is thus: they make an alley of about two hundred feet in length, where a very smooth clayey ground is laid, which when dry is very hard: they play two together having each a straight pole about fifteen feet long; one holds a stone which is in the shape of a truck, which he throws before him over this alley, and the instant of its departure, they set off and run; in running they cast their poles after the stone; he that did not throw it endeavors to hit it; the other strives to strike the pole of his antagonist in its flight so as to prevent the pole of his opponent hitting the stone. If the first should strike the stone he counts one for it, and if the other by the dexterity of his cast should prevent the pole of his opponent hitting the stone, he counts one, but should both miss their aim the throw is renewed."

Le Page du Pratz [Footnote: Histoire de la Louisiane, Paris, 1738, Vol. III, p. 2.] describes the game as practised among the Natchez. He calls it "*Le Jeu de la Perche* which would be better named *de la crosse*." Dumont who was stationed at Natchez and also on the Yazoo, describes the game and speaks of it as "La Crosse." [Footnote: Memoires Historiques sur la Louisiane, Paris, 1753, Vol. I, p. 202.]

Adair is correct when he speaks of the antiquity of this game. When he dwells upon the fact that these stones are handed down from generation to generation, as the property of the village, he brings these tribes close to the mound dwellers. Sanier, [Footnote: Ancient Monuments of the Mississippi Valley, p. 223.] speaking of discoidal stones, found in the mounds, says, "It is known that among the Indian tribes of the Ohio and along the Gulf, such stones were in common use in certain favorite games." Lucien Carr [Footnote: 10th Annual Report Peabody Museum, p. 93. See also Schoolcraft's Indian tribes, Vol. I, p. 83.] describes and pictures a chunkee stone from Ely Mound, Va. Lewis and Clarke [Footnote: Lewis and Clarke's Expedition, Phila, 1814, Vol. I, p. 143.] describe the game as played among the Mandans. This tribe had a wooden platform prepared on the ground between two of their lodges. Along this platform the stone ring was rolled and the sticks were slid along the floor in pursuit of it. Catlin [Footnote: Vol. I, p. 132 *et seq.* Dorsey describes two forms of the game in use among the Omahas: "shooting at the rolling wheel" and "stick and ring" Third Annual Report. Bureau of Ethnology, pp. 335-336. cf. Travels in the Interior of America, in the years 1809, 1810 and 1811, by John Bradbury, p. 126.] describes the game as played by the same tribe. They had a carefully prepared pavement of clay on which they played. The "Tchunkee" sticks were marked with bits of leather and the counts of the game were affected by the position of the leather on or near which the ring lodged. The Mojaves are accustomed to play a similar game which has been described under the name "Hoop and Pole". [Footnote: Lieut. A. W. Whipple in Pac. R. R. Rep.. Vol. III, p. 114; Harper's Mag., Vol. XVII, p. 463; Domenech. Vol. II, p. 197; H. H. Bancroft's Native Races, Vol. I, p. 393, p. 517 and note 133. The Martial Experiences of the California Volunteers by Edward Carlsen, Overland, Vol. VII, No. 41. 2nd Series, p. 494.] A similar game was played by the Navajoes. [Footnote: Major E. A. Backus in Schoolcraft. Vol. IV, p. 214.]

The Yumas played a game with two poles fifteen feet long and a ring a few inches in diameter. [Footnote: W. H. Emory, U. S. and Mexican Boundary Survey, Vol. I, p. 111.] Kane [Footnote: Kane's Wanderings, p. 310; H. H. Bancroft's Native Races, Vol. I, p. 280.] says that the Chualpays at Fort Colville on the Columbia "have a game which they call '*Alkollock*,' which requires considerable skill. A smooth, level piece of ground is chosen, and a slight barrier of a couple of sticks placed lengthwise is laid at each end of the chosen spot, being from forty to fifty feet apart and only a few inches high. The two players, stripped naked, are armed with a very slight spear, about three feet long, and finely pointed with bone; one of them takes a ring made of bone or some heavy wood and wound with cord. The ring is about three inches in diameter, on the inner circumference of which are fastened six beads of different colors, at equal distances, to each of which a separate value is attached. The ring is then rolled along the ground to one of the barriers and is followed at the distance of two or three yards by the players, and as the ring strikes the barrier and is falling on its side, the spears are thrown, so that the ring may fall on them. If any one of the spears should be covered by the ring, the owner counts according to the colored bead on it. But it generally happens from the dexterity of the players that the ring covers both spears and each counts according to the color of the beads above his spear. They then play towards the other barrier, and so on until one party has obtained the number agreed upon for the game."

In his "Life among the Apaches," [Footnote: Life among the Apaches by John C. Cremony, p. 302.] Colonel Cremony describes the hoop and pole game as played by the Apaches. With them the pole is marked with divisions throughout its whole length and these divisions are stained different colors. The object of the game is to make the hoop fall upon the pole as near the butt as possible, graduated values being applied to the different divisions of the pole. The women are not permitted to approach within a hundred yards while the game is going on. [Transcriber's Note: Lengthy footnote relocated to chapter end.] Those who have described this game in the various forms in which it has been presented dwell upon the fact that it taxed the strength, activity and skill of the players. In this respect it rivalled lacrosse. In geographical range the territory in which it was domesticated was nearly the same.

There are many, doubtless, who would decline to recognize the discoidal stones of the mounds as chunkee stones, but it can not be denied that the "*netlecawaw*" of the Cherokees [Footnote: Timberlake p. 77.], the "hoop and pole" of the Mojaves and Apaches [Footnote: Whipple, Pac. R. R. Rep., Vol. III, p. 114. Cremony, p. 302, Harper's Mag. Vol. XVII, p.

463.], the second form of "spear and ring" described by Domenech, [Footnote: Domenech, Vol. II, p. 197.] the "*alkollock*" of the Chualpays [Footnote: Kane's Wanderings, p. 310.] and the chunkee of Romans and Adair are the same game. The change from the discoidal stone to the ring; the different materials of which the ring is made, whether of stone, [Footnote: Lewis and Clarke, Vol. I, p. 143; Catlin, Vol. I, p. 132.] of bone, [Footnote: Kane's Wanderings, p. 310.], of wood, [Footnote: Cremony, p. 302.] or of cord; [Footnote: Whipple, Pac. R. R. Rep., Vol. III, p. 114.] whether wound with cord [Footnote: Kane's Wanderings, p. 310.] or plain; the different lengths of the spears varying from three feet [Footnote: Ibid.] to ten feet [Footnote: Timberlake, p. 77; Cremony, p. 302.] and even reaching fifteen feet in length among the Mojaves; [Footnote: Whipple, Pac. R. R. Rep., Vol. III, p. 114.] the different markings of the spear [Footnote: Cremony, p. 302; Domenech, Vol. II, p. 197; Timberlake, p. 77.] and the ring; [Footnote: Kane's Wanderings, p. 310.] the different ways of preparing the ground, whether tamping with clay, [Footnote: Catlin, Vol., I, p. 132.] or flooring with timber, [Footnote: Lewis and Clarke, Vol. I, p. 148.] or simply removing the vegetation, [Footnote: Domenech, Vol. II, p. 197.] - all these minor differences are of little consequence. The striking fact remains that this great number of tribes, so widely separated, all played a game in which the principal requirements were, that a small circular disk should be rolled rapidly along a prepared surface and that prepared wooden implements, similar to spears, should be launched at the disk while in motion or just at the time when it stopped. Like lacrosse, it was made use of as an opportunity for gambling, but owing to the restriction of the ground on which it could be played, the number of players were limited, and to that extent the interest in the contests and the excitement attendant upon them were proportionally reduced.

[Relocated Footnote: The Hawaiians were accustomed to hurl a piece of hard lava along narrow trenches prepared for the purpose. The stone which was called Maika closely resembled a chunkee stone. It is described as being in the shape of a small wheel or roller, three inches in diameter and an inch and a half thick, very smooth and highly polished. This game appears to have been limited to a contest of skill in rolling or hurling the stone itself. The additional interest which was given by hurling the spears at it while in motion was wanting. Narrative of the U. S. Exploring Expedition by Charles Wilkes, London, 1815, Vol. IV, p. 35.]

OTHER ATHLETIC GAMES.

In addition to the games of lacrosse, platter or dice, straws and chunkee, there were other games, some of an athletic nature, some purely of chance, which observers have described, some of which are mentioned only in limited areas, while others, like the games above mentioned, were played by Indians scattered over a wide territory and apparently having but little in common. Some of these games were but modified forms of those which have been already described. Such, for instance, is a game of ball which is described by Lafitau [Footnote: Lafitau, Vol. II, p. 353.]and by Charlevoix. [Footnote: Charlevoix, Vol. III, p. 319.] This closely resembled lacrosse in its general methods of play, but as no rackets were used, it was less dangerous and less exciting. Goals were erected at each end of the field, separated by five hundred paces according to Lafitau. The players were divided into sides. The ball was tossed into the air in the centre of the field. When it came down the players of each side strove to catch it. He who was successful ran in the direction of the goal which he wished to reach. The players of the opposite side pursued him and did what they could to prevent him from accomplishing his object. When it was evident that the runner could gain no more ground, he would pass the ball, if possible, to some player upon the same side and his success in accomplishing this was dependent

largely upon his skill. The game is probably not so old as lacrosse, for the ball is described as being larger and softer than the one used in lacrosse, thus indicating that it belonged to the period when the stuffed deer-skin ball was used in
that game.

Both Dumont and Le Page du Pratz describe this game with this difference, [Footnote: Dumont, Vol. I, p. 201, LePage, Vol. I, p. 378.] that the ball, according to their descriptions, was incessantly tossed in the air. Romans says that this game was played among the women; and Lafitau, who describes it separately, adds that in this form it was only played by girls. He also says that the Abenakis indulged in a similar game, using an inflated bladder for a ball; and that the Florida Indians fixed a willow cage upon a pole in such a way that it could revolve and tried to hit it with a ball so as to make it turn several times. [Footnote: Lafitau. Vol. II, p. 158.]

Joutel in his historical journal describes a curious game as follows: "Taking a short stick, very smooth and greased that it may be the harder to hold it fast, one of the elders throws it as far as he can. The young men run after it, snatch it from each other, and at last, he who remains possessed of it has the first lot." [Footnote: French's Historical Collections of Louisiana, Vol. I, p. 188; Sanford's History of the United States before the Revolution, p. clxxxii.]

Football is found at the north. Ogilby [Footnote: Ogilby, Book II, Chap. II, p. 156. See also Smith's Narrative, p. 77.] says: "Their goals are a mile long placed on the sands, which are as even as a board; their ball is no bigger than a hand ball, which sometimes they mount in the air with their naked feet, sometimes it is swayed by the multitude, sometimes also it is two days before they get a goal, then they mark the ground they win, and begin there the next day. Before they come to this sport they paint themselves, even as when they go to war." At the south it was "likewise a favorite manly diversion with them." [Footnote: Bartram, p. 509.]

Certain forms of ball-play which were neither lacrosse nor chunkee, but which resembled these games were found in different localities. Such for instance is the game which Catlin [Footnote: Vol. II, p. 146.] saw played by the Sioux women. Two balls were connected with a string a foot and a half long. Each woman was armed with a stick. They were divided into equal sides. Goals were erected and the play was in some respects like lacrosse. Stakes were wagered on the game. This game is also-described by Domenech, [Footnote: Vol. II, p. 196.] who says the women wore a special costume which left the limbs free and that the game was "unbecoming and indecent." Powers [Footnote: Contribution to North American Ethnology, Vol. III, p. 383.] found a game among the Nishinams, on the western slope of the Sierra Nevada, not far from Sacramento, which in some respects also resembled lacrosse. He says "The '*Ti'-kel*' is the only really robust and athletic game they use, and is played by a large company of men and boys. The piece [Footnote: The equivalent in the game, of the ball in lacrosse.] is made of raw-hide or nowadays of strong cloth, and is shaped like a small dumb-bell. It is laid in the centre of a wide, level space of ground, in a furrow, hollowed out a few inches in depth. Two parallel lines are drawn equidistant from it, a few paces apart, and along these lines the opposing parties, equal in strength, range themselves. Each player is equipped with a slight, strong staff, from four to six feet long. The two champions of the party take their stations on opposite sides of the piece, which is thrown into the air, caught on the staff of one of the others, and hurled by him in the direction of his antagonist's goal. With this send-off there ensues a wild chase and a hustle, pell-mell, higgledy-piggledy, each party striving to bowl the piece over the other's goal. These goals are several hundred yards apart.

In an article in the Overland Monthly, [Footnote: Vol. II, p. 433. See also Smith's Narrative, p. 77.] A. W. Chase describes a game in vogue among the Oregon Indians which he says was identical with hockey, as follows: "Sides being chosen, each endeavors to drive a hard ball of pine wood around a stake and in different directions; stripped to the buff, they display great activity and strength, whacking away at each other's shins, if they are in the way, with a refreshing disregard of bruises. The squaws assist in the performance by beating drums and keeping up a monotonous chant." In the first of the two games of "spear and ring," described by Domenech, [Footnote: Vol. II, pp. 197-8.] the players are divided into sides. The stone ring, about three inches in diameter, is fixed upright on the chosen ground, and players two at a time, one from each side, endeavor to throw their spears through the ring. The spears are marked along their length with little shields or bits of leather, and the count is affected by the number of these that pass through the ring. He also mentions a game [Footnote: He does not give his authority for this game. He has evidently copied in his book from other writers, but seldom indicates whether his descriptions are based upon personal observation or quoted.] among the Natchez in which the ring was a "huge stone" and the spear a "stick of the shape of a bat."

If we classify Domenech's first game of "spear and ring" among those which resemble chunkee, rather than as a form of chunkee itself, we shall probably be compelled to pursue the same course with Morgan's game of "javelin" to which we have already alluded. [Footnote: League of the Iroquois, p. 300.] In this game the players divided into sides. Each player had an agreed number of javelins. The ring, which was either a hoop or made solid like a wheel by winding with splints, was about eight inches in diameter. The players on one side were arranged in a line and the hoop was rolled before them. They hurled their javelins. The count of the game was kept by a forfeiture of javelins. Such as hit the mark were safe, but the javelins which did not hit were passed to the players of the other side who then had an opportunity to throw them at the hoop from the same spot. If these players were successful the javelins were forfeited and laid out of the play. If, however, they in turn failed the javelins were returned to their original owners. The hoop was then rolled by the other side and the process continued until one of the sides had forfeited all their javelins.

OTHER GAMES OF CHANCE.

There was diversity in the forms of the games of simple chance as well as in the athletic games, and besides those which have been already described, the Indians on the Pacific Coast had a great variety of games, or forms of the same game, in which, in addition to the element of chance involved in determining the numbers or positions of certain sticks or counters, there was also an opportunity for the player who was manipulating them to deceive by dexterous sleight of hand. The simplest form in which this is found is guessing in which hand a small stone or bone is held. It would hardly seem that this artless effort could be transformed into an amusing and exciting game; yet it has attracted the attention of all travellers, and scarcely any writer, who treats of the habits of the Pacific coast Indian, fails to give a full account of this simple game. Lewis and Clarke, [Footnote: Lewis and Clarke, Vol. II, 140; and also II, 94.] when writing about the Indians near the mouth of the Columbia, say: "The games are of two kinds. In the first, one of the company assumes the office of banker and plays against the rest. He takes a small stone, about the size of a bean, which he shifts from one hand to another with great dexterity, repeating at the same time a song adapted to the game and which serves to divert the attention of the company, till having agreed on the stakes, he holds out his hands, and the antagonist wins or loses as he succeeds or fails at guessing in which hand the stone is. After the banker has lost his money or whenever he is tired, the stone is transferred to another, who in turn challenges the rest of the company. [Footnote: See also, Adventures on the Columbia River, by Ross Cox. p. 158; The Oregon Territory, by John Dunn, p. 93; Four Years in British Columbia, by Commander R. C. Mayne, p. 273; it was played by the Comanches in Texas with a bullet, Robert S. Neighbors in Schoolcraft, Vol. II, p. 134; by the Twanas with one or two bones, Bulletin U. S. Geol. Survey, Vol. III, No. 1, p. 89, Rev. M. Eels.] In the account given by George Gibbs [Footnote: Contributions to North American Ethnology, Vol. I, p. 206.] the count of the game among the tribes of western Washington and northwestern Oregon, was kept by means of sticks. Each side took five or ten small sticks, one of which was passed to the winner on each guess, and the game was ended when the pile of one side was exhausted. According to him, "The backers of the party manipulating keep up a constant drumming with sticks on their paddles which lie before them, singing an incantation to attract good fortune." Powers describes another form into which the game developed among the Indians of central California. It is "played with a bit of wood or a pebble which is shaken in the hand, and then the hand closed upon it. The opponent guesses which finger (a thumb is a finger with them) it is under and scores one if he hits, or the other scores if he misses. They keep tally with eight counters." [Footnote: Contributions to North American Ethnology, Vol. III, pp. 332-3.]

Schwatka, in his recent exploration of the Yukon found this game among the Chilkats. It was called *la-hell*. Two bones were used. One was the king and one the queen. His packers gambled in guessing at the bones every afternoon and evening after reaching camp. [Footnote: Along Alaska's Great River. By Frederic Schwatka, p. 71.]

The simplicity of the game was modified by the introduction of similar articles in each hand, the question to be decided being in which hand one of them having a specified mark should be found. Kane [Footnote: Kane's Wanderings, p. 189.] thus describes such a game among the Chinooks: "Their games are few. The one most generally played amongst them consists in holding in each hand a small stick, the thickness of a goose quill, and about an inch and one-half in length, one plain, the other distinguished by a little thread wound round it, the opposite party being required to guess in which hand the marked stick is to be found. A Chinook will play at this simple game for days and nights together, until he has gambled away everything he possesses, even to his wife." [Footnote: See also Overland, Vol. IV, p. 163, Powers, H. H. Bancroft's Native Races, Vol. I n 244 Clay balls are sometimes used, Ibid, Vol. I, p. 353, The Northwest Coast James G Swan, p. 158, Montana as it is Granville Stuart, p. 71.]

Among the Utahs this form of the game was common: "A row of players consisting of five or six or a dozen men is arranged on either side of the tent facing each other. Before each man is placed a bundle of small twigs or sticks each six or eight inches in length and pointed at one end. Every tete-a-tete couple is provided with two cylindrical bone dice carefully fashioned and highly polished which measure about two inches in length and half an inch in diameter, one being white and the other black, or sometimes ornamented with a black band." At the rear, musicians were seated who during the game beat upon rude drums. [Footnote: Edwin R Baker in the American Naturalist, June, 1877, Vol. XI, p. 551.] In this game it will be noticed that the players paired off and apparently each man played for himself.

Still another element is introduced in another form of the game, which increases the opportunity afforded the one who manipulates the bones for dexterity. This form of the game is repeatedly alluded to by Powers. While relating the habits and customs of the Gualala, whose homes were near Fort Ross, he describes what he calls the gambling game of "*wi* and *tep*" and says that one description with slight variations will answer for nearly all the tribes of central and southern California. After describing the making up of the pool of stakes, he adds: "They gamble with four cylinders of bone about two inches long, two of which are plain, and two marked with rings and strings tied round the middle. The game is conducted by four old and experienced men, frequently grey heads, two for each party, squatting on their knees on opposite sides of the fire. They have before them a quantity of fine dry grass, and with their hands in rapid and juggling motions before and behind them, they roll up each piece of bone in a little ball and the opposite party presently guess in which hand is the marked bone. Generally only one guesses at a time, which he does with the word '*lep*' (marked one), and '*wi*' (plain one). If he guesses right for both players, they simply toss the bones over to him and his partner, and nothing is scored on either side. If he guesses right for one and wrong for the other, the one for whom he guessed right is 'out', but his partner rolls up the bones for another trial, and the guesser forfeits to them one of his twelve counters. If he guesses wrong for both, they still keep on and he forfeits two counters. There are only twelve counters and when they have been all won over to one side or the other, the game is ended. [Footnote: Powers in Contributions to North American Ethnology, Vol. III, pp. 90-152; 189-332.] Sometimes the same game was played without going through the formality of wrapping the pieces in grass, simply shaking them in the hands as a preliminary for the guessing. [Footnote: Contributions to North American Ethnology, Vol. III, 332; Alexander Ross's Adventures, pp. 308, 309.]

A slightly different method prevails among the Indians of Washington and northwestern Oregon. Ten disks of hard wood, each about the diameter of a Mexican dollar and somewhat thicker, are used. "One of these is marked and called the chief. A smooth mat is spread on the ground, at the ends of which the opposing players are seated, their friends on either side, who are provided with the requisites for a noise as in the other case. The party holding the disks has a bundle of the fibres of the cedar bark, in which he envelops them, and after rolling them about, tears the bundle into two parts, his opponent guessing in which bundle the chief lies." [Footnote: Contributions to North American Ethnology, Gibbs, Vol. I, p. 206.] The same game is described by Kane, except that the counters, instead of being wrapped in one bundle which is afterward torn in two, are originally wrapped in two bundles. [Footnote: Kane's Wanderings, p. 189; Swan's Northwest Coast, p. 157, Eels in Bulletin U.S.G. Surv., Vol. III, No. 1.]

Still another complication of the guessing game was described by Mayne. [Footnote: Mayne's British Columbia, p. 275.] Blankets were spread upon the ground on which sawdust was spread about an inch thick. In this was placed the counter, a piece of bone or iron about the size of a half a crown, and one of the players shuffled it about, the others in turn guessing where it was.

The game of "moccasin" was but a modification of this game. As described by Philander Prescott three moccasins were used in this game by the Dacotas. The bone or stick was slipped from one to another of the moccasins by the manipulators, and the others had to guess in which moccasin it was to be found. Simple as this description seems, the men would divide into sides, playing against each other, and accompanying the game with singing. [Footnote: Schoolcraft, Vol. IV, p. 64; Domenech, Vol. II, p. 192.]

Among the Zunis, the guessing game was exalted to the nature of a sacred festival. Frank H. Cushing [Footnote: The Century, Vol. XXVI, p. 37.] gives the following account of its practice. "One morning the two chief priests of the bow climbed to the top of the houses, and just at sunrise called out a 'prayer message' from the mount-environed gods. Eight players went into a *kli-wi-lain* to fast, and four days later issued forth, bearing four large wooden tubes, a ball of stone, and a bundle of thirty-six counting straws. With great ceremony, many prayers and incantations, the tubes were deposited on two mock mountains of sand, either side of the 'grand plaza.' A crowd began to gather. Larger and noisier it grew, until it became a surging, clamorous, black mass. Gradually two piles of fabrics, - vessels, silver ornaments, necklaces, embroideries, and symbols representing horses, cattle and sheep - grow to large proportions. Women gathered on the roofs around, wildly stretching forth articles for betting, until one of the presiding priests called out a brief message. The crowd became silent. A booth was raised, under which two of ho players retired; and when it was removed the four tubes were standing on the mound of sand. A song and dance began. One by one three of the four opposing players were summoned to guess under which tube the ball was hidden. At each guess the cries of the opposing party became deafening, and the mock struggles approached the violence of combat. The last guesser found the ball; and as he victoriously carried the latter and the tubes across to his own mound, his side scored ten. The process was repeated. The second guesser found the ball; his side scored fifteen setting the others back five. The counts, numbered one hundred; but so complicated were the winnings and losings on both sides, with each guess of either, that hour after hour the game went on, and night closed in. Fires were built in the plaza, cigarettes were lighted, but still the game continued. Noisier and noisier grew the dancers; more and more insulting and defiant their songs and epithets to the opposing crowd, until they fairly gnashed their teeth at one another, but no blows. Day dawned upon the still uncertain contest; nor was it until the sun again touched the western horizon, that the hoarse, still defiant voices died away, and the victorious party bore off their mountains of gifts from the gods." The picturesque description of Cushing brings before our eyes the guessing game in its highest form of development. Among the tribes of the East, if it had a home at all, it was practised in such an inobtrusive way as not to attract the attention of writers who have described their habits and customs. The nearest approach to it which we can find is a guessing game described by Hennepin, as follows: "They take kernels of Indian corn or something of the kind, then they put some in one hand, and ask how many there are. The one who guesses wins."

Mackenzie [Footnote: Alexander Mackenzie's Voyages in 1789 and 1893 London, 1801, p. 311.] fell in with some Indians near the Pacific coast who travelled with him a short distance. They carried with them the implements for gambling. Their game was different from the guessing games which have been heretofore described. "There were two players and each had a bundle of about fifty small sticks neatly polished, of the size of a quill, and five inches long. A certain number of their sticks had red lines round them and as many of these as one of the players might find convenient were curiously rolled up in dried grass, and according to the judgment of his antagonist respecting their number and marks he lost or won."

The same game was seen at Queen Charlotte Islands by Francis Poole. [Footnote: Queen Charlotte Island, a narrative etc., p. 25.] He says there were in this game from "forty to fifty round pins or pieces of wood, five inches long by one-eighth of an inch thick, painted in black and blue rings and beautifully polished." These pins were divided into two heaps under cover of bark fibre and the opposite player guessed odd or even for one of the piles.

CONTESTS OF SKILL.

Lewis and Clarke [Footnote: Vol. II, p. 140.] describe a game among the Oregon Indians which can neither be called an athletic game nor a game of chance, but which seems to have been a simple contest of skill. "Two pins are placed on the floor, about the distance of a foot from each other, and a small hole made behind them. The players then go about ten feet from the hole, into which they try to roll a small piece, resembling the men used at draughts; if they succeed in putting it into the hole, they win the stake; if the piece rolls between the pins, but does not go into the hole, nothing is won or lost; but the wager is wholly lost if the chequer rolls outside the pins."

Morgan [Footnote: League of the Iroquois, p. 303.] describes a winter contest of skill among the Iroquois, which he calls snow-snake. The so-called snakes were made of hickory. They were from five to seven feet in length, a quarter of an inch in thickness, tapering from an inch in width at the head to about half an inch at the tail. The head was round, turned up slightly and weighted with lead. This implement was shot along the snow crust, by hand, with great speed, and a point in the game was gained by the snake which ran the greatest distance. When there were a number of players divided into sides, if there were two, three or more snakes of the same side which were in advance of the snakes of the other side, all such counted. Such contests usually took place between tribes and aroused a great degree of spirit and the usual amount of betting. In simpler form, Sagard Theodat describes this kind of amusement.

OTHER AMUSEMENTS OF WOMEN AND CHILDREN.

Under the name of "*Fuseaux*," La Potherie [Footnote: Vol. III, p. 24.] describes a similar winter game of the children. He further says the women only played at platter or dice. The children played at lacrosse, seldom at platter. We have seen that the women in some parts of the country joined in the lacrosse games. Sometimes they played it by themselves and sometimes they played other ball games which closely resemble that game. Romans describes a woman's game in which they tossed up a ball which was to be caught before it reached the ground; but in the meantime the one who tossed it had to pick up a small stick from the ground.

The women of the Natchez, [Footnote: Le Page du Pratz, Vol. III, p. 2, Domenech, Vol. II, p. 192.] according to Le Page du Pratz, played with three pieces of cane, each eight or nine inches long, flat on one side and convex on the other with engravings on the convex side. Two were held in the open palm of the left hand and the third was dropped round side down upon the ends of the two, so that all would fall to the ground. If two convex surfaces came up the player won. He also says, and in this Romans concurs, that the women were very reluctant to be seen while playing.

Among the Natchez, the young girls played ball with a deer-skin ball stuffed with Spanish moss. Other than that they seemed to him to have no games. [Footnote: Le Page du Pratz, Vol. III, p. 2.] The young Choctaws, according to Romans, engaged in wrestling, running, heaving and lifting great weights and playing ball. Hennepin says, "the children play with bows and with two sticks, one large and one small. They hold the little one in the left, and the larger one in the right hand, then with the larger one they make the smaller one fly up in the air, and another runs after it, and throws it at the one who sprang it. They also make a ball of flags or corn leaves, which they throw in the air and catch on the end of a pointed stick." Powers [Footnote: Contributions to North American Ethnology. Vol. III, p. 331.] describes a game among the children of the Nishinams which consisted in tossing bunches of clover from one to another, and another in which the boys placed themselves upon three bases and tossed a ball across from one to the other. Points were won as in base ball by running bases, if possible, without being put out by the one who at the time had the ball. The Choctaw [Footnote: Romans, p. 70, Bossu, Vol. I, p. 308.] boys made use of a cane stalk, eight or nine feet in length, from which the obstructions at the joints had been removed, much as boys use what is called a putty blower. The Zuni children are said to play checkers with fragments of pottery on flat stones. [Footnote: The Century, Vol. XXVI, p. 28, Cushing.]

Running matches, swimming, wrestling, the simple ball-games which are hinted at rather than described, practice in archery and hurling the spear or javelin, furnished the Indian youth with such amusements as could be derived outside the contests in which his elders participated. Most of these latter were so simple as to be easily understood by the very young, and we can readily comprehend how deeply the vice of gambling must have been instilled in their minds, when they saw it inaugurated with such solemn ceremonials and participated in with such furor by their elders.

Our information concerning the habits of the Indians comes from a variety of sources. Some of it is of very recent date, especially that which deals with the Indians of the Pacific coast. The early Relations of the French Fathers were faithful, and, as a rule, intelligent records of events which the priests themselves witnessed. The accounts of the French and Indian traders and travelers are neither as accurate nor as reliable as those contained in the Relations. Some of these authors faithfully recorded what they saw; others wrote to make books. They differ widely in value as authorities and must be judged upon their individual merits.

Much of our information concerning the manners and customs of the natives of the Pacific coast is derived from the publications of our national government. The reports which are collated in these documents are from a great number of observers and are not uniform in character, but many of them have great value. As a whole, the work was well done and in a scientific manner.

The narration of the different games tells its own story. Lacrosse is found throughout the country; platter or dice is distributed over an area of equal extent; chunkee was a southern and western game; straws a northern game with traces of its existence in the west; the guessing game was apparently a western game. Everywhere, gambling prevailed to the most shocking extent.

There are writers who seek to reduce the impressions of the extravagance indulged in by the Indians at these games. The concurrence of testimony is to the effect that there was no limit to which they would not go. Their last blanket or bead, the clothing on their backs, their wives and children, their own liberty were sometimes hazarded; and if the chances of the game went against them the penalty was paid with unflinching firmness. The delivery of the wagered wives, Lescarbot tells us, was not always accomplished with ease, but the attempt would be faithfully made and probably was often successful. Self-contained as these people ordinarily were, it is not a matter of surprise that the weaker among them should have been led to these lengths of extravagance, under the high pressure of excitement which was deliberately maintained during the progress of their games. [Transcriber's Note: Lengthy footnote relocated to chapter end.] From one end of the land to the other these scenes were ushered in with ceremonies calculated to increase their importance and to awaken the interest of the spectators. The methods used were the same among the confederations of the north and of the south; among the wandering tribes of the interior; among the dwellers in the Pueblos; and among the slothful natives of the Pacific coast.

The scene described by Cushing, where, at the summons of the "prayer-message," the Zunis gathered upon the house-tops and swarmed in the Plaza, to hazard their property, amid prayers and incantations, upon a guess under which tube the ball was concealed, is widely different from that depicted by the Jesuit Fathers in Canada, where the swarthy Hurons assembled in the Council House at the call of the medicine man and in the presence of the sick man,

Andrew McFarland Davis

wagered their beads and skins, upon the cast of the dice. It differs equally from the scene which travellers have brought before our eyes, of the Chinooks, beating upon their paddles and moaning forth their monotonous chants, while gathered in a ring about the player, who with dexterous passes and strange contortions manipulated the stone and thus added zest to the guess which was to determine the ownership of the property staked upon the game. The resemblances in these scenes are, however, far more striking than the differences. Climate and topography determine the one. Race characteristics are to be found in the other.

[Relocated Footnote: The following extracts will illustrate these points: They will bet all they have, even to their wives. It is true, however, that the delivery of the wagered women is not easy. They mock the winners and point their fingers at them (Lescarbot, Vol. III, p. 754); all that they possess, so that if unfortunate, as sometimes has happened, they return home as naked as your hand (Lalemant, Relation, 1639); their goods, their wives, their children (Ferland Vol. I, p. 134); some have been known to stake their liberty for a time (Charlevoix, Vol. III, 319); have been known to stake their liberty upon the issue of these games, offering themselves to their opponents in case they get beaten (Catlin, Vol. I, p. 132); I have known several of them to gamble their liberty away (Lawson, p. 176); a Canadian Indian lost his wife and family to a Frenchman (Sagard Theodat, Histoire du Canada, Vol. I, p. 243); they wager their wives (A. Colquhon Grant, Journal Royal Geog. Soc., London, Vol. XXVII, p. 299); their wives and children (Irving's Astorla, Vol. II, p. 91); their liberty (Parker's Journal of an Exploring Tour, pp. 249-50); Domenech has never known men to bet their wives (Vol. II, p. 191); women bet as well as men (Romans, p. 79; Am. Naturalist, Vol. XI, No. 6, 551); Philander Prescott (Schoolcraft, Vol. IV, p. 64); Cushing (Century, Vol. XXVI, p. 28); the liberty of a woman wagered by herself (Lalemant, Relation 1639); women are never seen to bet (Le Page du Pratz, Vol. III, p. 2; Mayne Br. Col., p. 276); rash gambling sometimes followed by suicide (Romans p. 79; Brebeuf, Relation 1686).]

www.ingramcontent.com/pod-product-compliance
Lightning Source LLC
Chambersburg PA
CBHW022128280326
41933CB00007B/600